LOVE

ESSENTIAL POETS SERIES 322

Canada Council for the Arts
Conseil des Arts du Canada

ONTARIO ARTS COUNCIL
CONSEIL DES ARTS DE L'ONTARIO
an Ontario government agency
un organisme du gouvernement de l'Ont

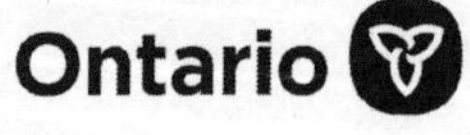

Canada

Guernica Editions Inc. acknowledges the support of the Canada Council for the Arts and the Ontario Arts Council. The Ontario Arts Council is an agency of the Government of Ontario.

We acknowledge the financial support of the Government of Canada.

MAX LAYTON

LOVE

GUERNICA
EDITIONS

TORONTO – BUFFALO – LANCASTER (U.K.)

2025

Copyright © 2025, Max Layton and Guernica Editions Inc.
All rights reserved. The use of any part of this publication, reproduced, transmitted in any form or by any means, electronic, mechanical, photocopying, recording or otherwise stored in a retrieval system, without the prior consent of the publisher is an infringement of the copyright law.
This material is protected by copyright law and may not be used for machine learning, AI training, or data mining without explicit written permission. This includes, but is not limited to, the use of text, images, and other content for the development of AI models.

Guernica Founder: Antonio D'Alfonso

Michael Mirolla, editor
Cover and interior design: Errol F. Richardson
Front cover painting: Gordon Rayner, Sr.

Guernica Editions Inc.
1241 Marble Rock Rd., Gananoque, (ON), Canada K7G 2V4
2250 Military Road, Tonawanda, N.Y. 14150-6000 U.S.A.
www.guernicaeditions.com

Distributors:
University of Toronto Press Distribution (UTP)
5201 Dufferin Street, Toronto (ON), Canada M3H 5T8
Independent Publishers Group (IPG)
814 N Franklin Street, Chicago, IL 60610, U.S.A.

First edition.
Printed in Canada.

Legal Deposit – Third Quarter
Library of Congress Catalogue Card Number: 2025937791
Library and Archives Canada Cataloguing in Publication
Title: Love / Max Layton.
Names: Layton, Max, 1946- author.
Series: Essential poets ; 322.
Description: Series statement: Essential poets series ; 322
Identifiers: Canadiana 20250203154 | ISBN 9781778490293 (softcover)
Subjects: LCGFT: Poetry.
Classification: LCC PS8573.A985 L68 2025 | DDC C811/.54—dc23

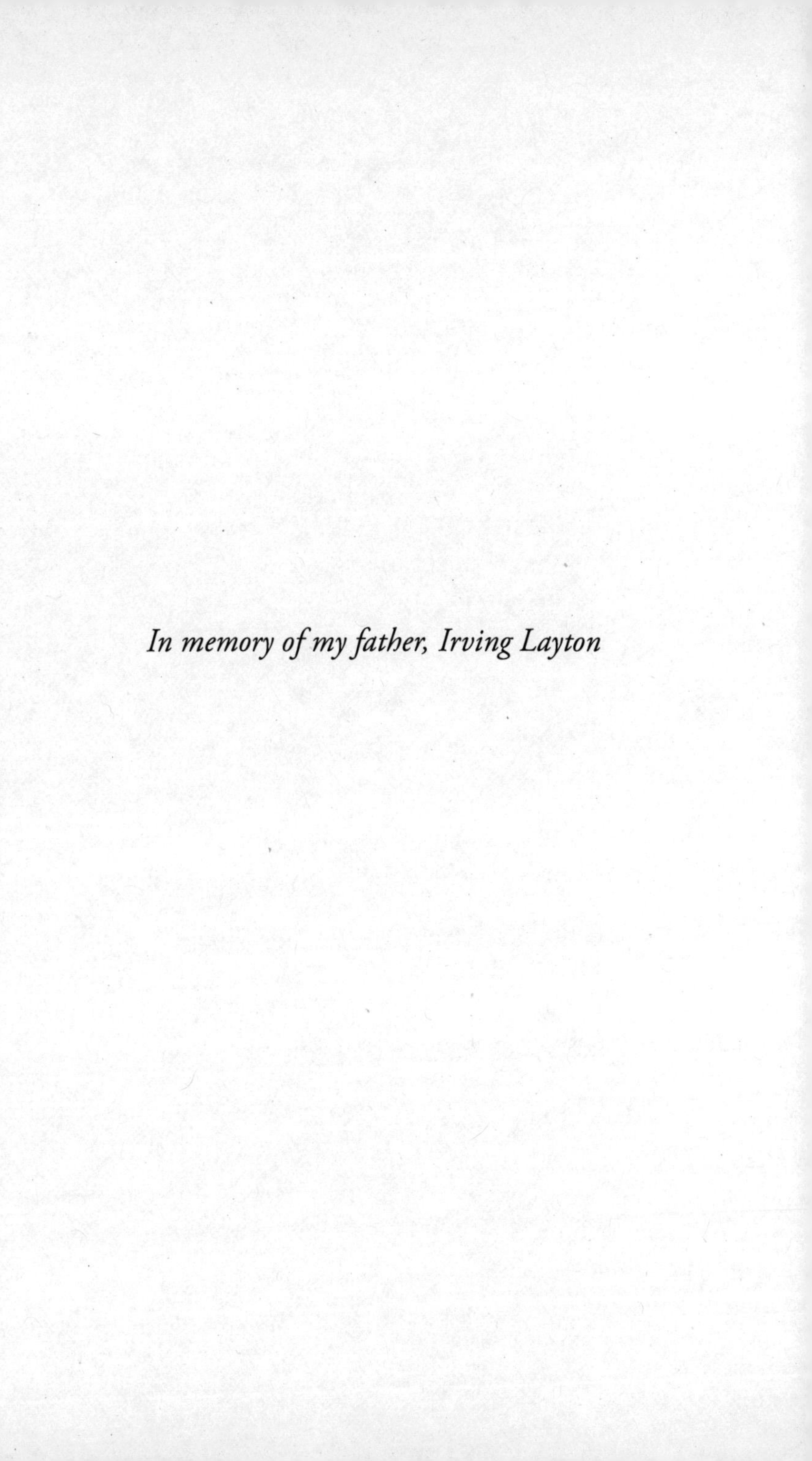

In memory of my father, Irving Layton

Contents

Harlequin Romance

That's me fifty years ago
Painted by a friend's late father

A professional illustrator

Me flattered when asked to pose for
The cover of a Harlequin Romance

My hair a thicket of brown
My Jewish nose straightened

Who'd have thought, a lifetime
Later, I'd be wearing a yarmulke
Of sun-speckled skin

The book was called *A Leaf In The Storm*

A title which, sappy as it sounds
Pretty well sums things up

I have no idea who the female was
I assume she too was flattered

She, the blue-eyed innocent
Waiting to be kissed

Me, the swarthy lover
Leaning in

Our imperfections brushed aside
Our separate lives joined forever

Bent Over

To this day if I straighten my legs
And bend over, I can still touch the
Floor with the palms of my hands

That's what you get for picking
Tobacco in Tillsonburg, Ontario
When you were fourteen years old

At six in the morning, the dew mixes
With tobacco juice and because you
Are bent over, it gets into your eyes

Each man in his own row, all of us
Half blind, bent over, trying to see
The leaves in the sand at our feet

Eventually the sun dries everything
And you think it is a blessing until
The heat makes it hard to breathe

Two rows over, a man falls to his
Knees

We pick him up and put him in the
Stone boat, actually a wooden sled
Pulled by a horse

We throw our armfuls of leaves into
The boat around him

The farmer arrives with a thermos of
Hot coffee

Are you crazy? somebody says

The farmer looks at the stone boat
And hauls the man out

He's crying and says he's done, that
He can't bend over anymore

The farmer tells the man to stand
Back-to-back and link elbows

When the farmer bends over
The man bends backwards and
Lets out a terrified shriek

But when the farmer puts him down
He says he can work again

After that, we bend over for each
Other at the end of each row

Sixty years later, I can still touch the
Floor with the palms of my hands

It's getting back up again that's not
As easy as it used to be

Please

I am seventeen and have only been in
The lumber camp a few days

But already I've noticed no one curses
More eloquently than a logger

They are poets of swearing

They swear rhythmically, heroically
Cutting a swear word in half, inserting
Another between

Except in the cookhouse

There everyone is on his best behaviour
There, once a day for a priceless hour
We are gentlemen

We say please and thank you

We've washed our hands
Some of us have even shaved

We sit at long tables, six men to a side

There's roast beef, sliced ham, chicken
Mounds of mashed potatoes, several
Different kinds of pies

On Saturday nights, there's all the steak
You can eat and scoops of ice cream

Sitting across from me is a Yugoslav, so
Broad-shouldered he has to turn sideways
To get through the cookhouse door

All of a sudden, the Yugoslav says to me:
Hey, Joo, passa da budda!

I almost swallowed my heart
The man had just called me a Jew

My first thought was, *How did he know?*

My second thought was, if I didn't fight
My life would become a living hell

My third thought was that he would crush
Me against his massive chest

What'd you say? I said as fiercely as I
Could

The Yugoslav's face turned a brilliant
Shade of red

Hey, joo, he stammered. *Passa da budda
Please!*

That's better! I said, and passed him
The butter

Buying Time

Six of us huddled between the tank
Tracks of a yarder, its black bottom
Shielding us from the pounding rain

All of us opening our lunch buckets
Unwrapping the sandwiches we made
Before breakfast

I have ham and cheese and a wedge
Of raisin pie

The best thing about a lumber camp is
The food

The smell of fresh-cut cedar and diesel
Fuel in our nostrils

Hot coffee steaming in our thermoses
A delicious cigarette afterwards

Beyond the metal cave of our shelter
It's been raining so hard you can't keep
A cigarette lit

Across from me is the guy who last
Week, for no reason, started chasing
Us with a 2x4

So we tied him to it, his arms out like
Christ on the cross

Until he stopped blubbering and promised
To behave

Now he is peering at his watch as if
Itching to get back to work

Engineer sets the time, the engineer
Says

Lunch is only over when the engineer
Climbs the ladder to his rainproof cab
On the yarder and sounds the horn

We understand he is trying to buy us
A few precious extra minutes

But then he groans and sluices the
Dregs of his coffee onto the ground

We close our lunch buckets, take
A few last drags on our cigarettes

The horn sounds

We hunch our shoulders and walk out
Into the rain

Fado

I am talking to the editor and owner of
The Hudson Bay Nugget

I tell him there are sixty Portuguese
Immigrants living in boxcars on a
Siding ten miles east of town

I tell him they are indentured labourers
Forced to work for the CNR

At below minimum wage

I tell him that, if fired, they are subject
To immediate deportation

I tell him the government is complicit in
What amounts to modern-day slavery

I ask for donations

Magazines
Playing cards
Used sports equipment

Incredibly, the story is picked up by the
Winnipeg Free Press and reprinted in
Newspapers across the country

Followed by outraged editorials

Two days later, there's a gigantic crate for
Me from the railroad's head office

Baseballs, volleyballs, footballs, tennis balls
Bats, gloves, rackets, nets, sets of horseshoes

***

That night, getting my hair cut in one of the
Boxcars, about twenty men come crowding in

They say they are grateful for what I have done
And somebody puts on a fado record

It is filled with the ancient sadness of the
Poor and dispossessed

An old man starts to sing
The liquor comes out
More voices join in

I am offered a drink

Fado, my barber says and tells me I look
Like the son he hasn't seen in seven years

He takes a photo off the wall above his bed
And holds it in front of my face as if it were
A mirror

My son, he says, and a tear lands on the back
Of my neck

Mechanic

At Aviron Technical School, when
I scored 100 on the final exam, I
Thought I was a genius

My teacher thought I was a
Genius

The garage that hired me
Thought I was a genius

The first car I worked on was a
Mini Cooper

Took me half the day to change
The oil filter

Then came the brakes

Took me the rest of the day to
Get the wheels off

Bolts rust
Nuts seize

There's an art to unscrewing things
Without stripping them

The guy in the next bay over could
Take one look at an engine and know
The tools he'd need

I had to walk to my toolbox over and
Over just to find the right wrench

The acetylene torch terrified me

One clumsy cut with its bright blue
Flame and the car above my head
Could explode

Was that the brake line?
Or the gas line?

That bastard in the next bay over
Would know

All he ever talked about was torque
And gear ratios

He was younger than me and had
Never been to technical school

Maybe I was a genius
But he was the mechanic

Book City

I loved being the owner of a bookstore

Compared to working in a lumber camp
There was very little chance a tree might
Fall on me

Zero chance of rain

And yet, when word got out that I owned
The place, there was a torrent, a deluge
Of willing young women

Understand, I was single and in my twenties
And my bookstore was located on the city's
Most fashionable street

Its Victorian pressed tin ceiling painted in
The most fashionable shibui trim

So, every night at closing time, there'd be
Two or three marriage-minded wannabes
Waiting in the aisles

Shyly asking if *Crime and Punishment* would
Be a good book to read

Or what did I think of Spinoza's philosophy?

I was amazed at how desperate they were to
Find a man with money who could talk about
Books

I thought a tree must have fallen on me

Being a Banker

I loved being a banker because the actor in me
Loved the starring role

I loved the big desk in the big office, the suits, the
Silk ties, the shoes as polished as my fingernails

I loved telling my secretary to book a flight to L.A.

I loved walking into somebody else's office wearing
My confident, all-knowing smile

I loved my well-rehearsed patter

There was only one problem: I didn't love money
I mean, other people's money

Or sports or the latest financial news or any of
The other things bankers love to talk about

I was terrified somebody would invite me to lunch
My script was good for no more than fifteen minutes

I told my friends I quit out of boredom
But the truth is, I needed a better writer

Teaching

I loved teaching
All classes, all grades

But my favourite was a truly unruly
Class of grade twelves who had made
Their previous teacher's life a misery

Boys mostly, two gang-bangers in
Their twenties

I told them I was the only man they
Would ever meet who had slept in a
Minefield and lived to tell about it

I told them I'd heard there were jobs
At the real King Solomon's Mines in
The Sinai Desert

I needed money so I hitch-hiked from
Tel Aviv down to Eilat on the Gulf of
Aqaba

It was dark by the time I arrived but I
Didn't mind because I wanted to see
The stars glinting on the Red Sea

So I walked along the beach until the
Lights of Eilat disappeared behind me

I knew Jordan must be straight ahead
But, as I rolled out my sleeping bag, I
Had no idea how close the border was

Anyway, in the morning when I woke
Up, I could see a—

The bell rang

The class begged me to finish the story
But I said only if they worked hard the
Next day

—I could see a gigantic sign which I
Must have walked past in the dark

And on that sign, on the Israeli side, in
Huge black letters in Hebrew and Arabic
And English and French, it said—

Again the bell rang and the class groaned

—The sign said:

STOP! DANGER!
MINEFIELD AHEAD!

Well, I had their attention and I kept the
Story going for weeks

I told them how I'd found myself standing
Beside a cracked asphalt road in the middle
Of the desert

A blue lake of mirage water was shimmering
All around me and coming towards me was a—

Sorry, no more story today: Bob was talking

The next day Bob had a spit lip and was
Remarkably quiet

My Dear Penis

I love you, my dear penis

The way you stood up for me
When I was down

And taught me the ins and outs
Of the Sixties sexual revolution

The way you so quickly became
Battle-hardened and soldiered on

Your conquistador's helmet forever
Ready to plunge headlong into the
Wilderness of an Amazon

The way, after a night of exhausting
Maneuvers, you still had the strength
To rise again at dawn

I remember the long marches, the
Evasive actions, the tactical retreats

The sudden, astonishing surrenders

Thanks to you, my dear penis
I saw, I conquered, I came

Hermaphrodite

I notice, lately, my dreams are coming
In 3D, like movies with me always at the
Centre of whatever's going on

Everything filmed from my point of view

Last night, for instance, I was my cousin
Louise, back when she was twenty and
Very, very beautiful

Honey-coloured hair and liquid eyes and
A mouth you'd want to stick your penis in

Which is what some smooth-skinned man
Was doing to me before he took me from
Behind

The thing is, I woke up with a huge erection

Of course, every writer is a hermaphrodite
Even Shakespeare must have been both
Romeo and Juliet

Anyway, that's what I tell myself and I find
I sleep much better

Scrabble

I don't always remember my dreams
But this one has stuck with me

Apparently, some young woman had
Swallowed a game of Scrabble

Words like LOVE and JEALOUSY and
HATE were now all jumbled together
Somewhere in her intestines

I was merely a vet but, once I opened
Her up, I could see how serious the
Problem was:

LOVE and HATE were joined at the E

While LOVE and JEALOUSY shared
L, O & E and were hopelessly intertwined

And so on

All the words strung together like a
Chain of conjoined twins

No way I could disentangle them

Best I could do was haul them out and
Reset the game on a brand new board

Of course, the woman was speechless
When she saw the scar she would have
To live with the rest of her life

Divorce

The rabbi revokes his benediction

The best man removes the velvet
Bag from under the bridegroom's
Boot

Then, so ceremoniously, he takes
Back the rings

The parents unfake their smiles

The bride walks backwards up
The aisle to the car

The groom drives backwards
Up the street

To the room they've shared for half
A year

Where several hundred meals are
Untasted and never cooked

Where the bed is made and unmade
And remade and the woman repacks
Her suitcases

While the young man lugs them back to
The other room down the hall

Where he had heard her singing to herself
So beautifully

Before they met, their eyes not yet
Shining

Half a Lifetime Ago

And here's the house I bought half
A lifetime ago

Not to mention the furniture, the stove
The fridge, the dish washer, the books
The two TVs

And the green filing cabinet for filing
Important memories

Birth certificate, marriage certificate
Divorce certificate, expired passports
Unpublished manuscripts

Letters from long lost friends
Yellowing photos of me as a kid

Also, the realtor's drone image of this
House I will probably die in

Here is my driveway and here is my roof

Here is my hill, my lawn, my favourite tree

And here, at the end of my property, is
The sixty foot slice of river I can swim in

But never step in twice

My Father in Winter

When I picture him, it is always
Summer and everything is green

So what is it about shovelling snow
That makes me think of him?

Especially when my shovel cuts
Square blocks in knee-high drifts?

Why is it then I hear his voice
Saying what a good job I've done?

Perhaps, I think, my snow-covered
Driveway is like a white sheet of
Paper and my truck is like a poem

But then I remember when I was
A kid, my father only sometimes
coming home

I remember working in the dark
In the middle of a Montreal winter

The snow deep and heavy

Me shovelling the driveway
Making the edges straight

Waiting for his car to pull in

My Father's Scarf

I love my father's scarf, the one
I got when he passed away

He had been in an old folks' home
And his watch, his rings, his silver
Bracelet, had all been stolen

Everything except his scarf

It was wide and long and made of fine
Warm wool striped in shades of red and
Blue and grey

When I wrapped it round my
Shoulders, it felt like my father's
Mantle had fallen upon me

Poems poured out of me

So you can imagine how I felt
When I lost it

I had just returned from a long
Walk and instantly ran back the
Way I'd come

Through rough brush and across
A creek at the bottom of a ravine

I was certain that that was where
The scarf would be

But it wasn't
So I ran on

Across a farmer's field and over
A hill onto a gravel path which led
Past a cemetery

Me thinking that perhaps this loss
Was meant to be, that perhaps it
Was a good thing

That perhaps my father's scarf had
Been a yoke around my neck

That perhaps, finally, I was free

When, just past the cemetery, there it
Was – my father's scarf lying in a heap
Of colour beside the trail

Books

The walls of my childhood home
Lined floor to ceiling with books

Multi-coloured tattered paperbacks
Rows of hardcovers stamped with
Gold lettering

Not collector's items but books my
Father actually read

Thousands of them

Him sitting all summer at a table
Under a willow tree in our back yard
A pile of books beside him

Later, *Read any good books lately?*
Was invariably his first question

And much later, before we moved
Him to the old folk's home, on a table
Beside him was always a pile of books

He said he was re-reading the essays
Of Montaigne

He said he was getting much more
Out of it than when he was young

It was half a year before I could
Visit him again

There, on the table beside him, was
The same pile of books

He said he was re-reading the essays of
Montaigne

He said he was getting much more
Out of it than when he was young

My Magic Window

The secret of my magic window
Has followed me since I was a kid

Though, being invisible, it has
Sometimes been hard to find

Times when I thought I had lost
It forever – years when I worked
As a banker and wore fancy suits

Right now, stretched across a path
In the woods, I feel it on my face

And then there's a silent whooshing
Sound when I pass through

I remember I was five or six when
The magic first happened

I had stolen a quarter from my mother's
Purse and had used it to buy a hotdog and
a pack of hockey cards, a black gumball
And a chocolate cigarillo

(Amazing what you could buy for a quarter
In those days)

Anyway, there I was on my tricycle wearing
My cowboy hat, my cap pistol at the ready
My cigarillo clenched between my teeth

When the magic window opened

And suddenly I was riding a palomino, the
Pistol in my hand firing real bullets, my hat
Flapping against my back, the smoke from
My cigarillo billowing in the rushing wind

In Another Life

In another life I might have worn leather leggings
and a
Deerskin jacket with fringes on my sleeves

In another life I might, mouth watering, have stalked
this goose
And shot it with an arrow

Might, in my hunger, have dashed across this river's
shallow moat
And brained the gander's nesting mate before she could
fly away

Anyway, I would have got the eggs

But, in this life, I am wearing blue jeans and Birkenstocks
and feel no hunger
Because my fridge is packed with food

In this life, I am sitting on a log smoking a cigarette and
thinking about
The wilderness this place must once have been

The gander, apparently asleep, is standing on one leg with
its head
Tucked under its wing

I say apparently asleep because, when I shift my
weight, his
Head swivels up and scans the sky for enemies

The bird relaxes, stares straight ahead
        at the river
I finish my cigarette and we both stare
        at the river

This goose and his mate have been coming here
        for years
Always nesting in the same place

I'd like to think they know I am a friend and that
        if attacked
A murderous, carnivorous ape would come to their
        defence

The goose puts his head back under his wing
        and I
Sit there guarding them

Windigo

I'd love to have been an
Aboriginal

A Cree warrior, say

Someone so close to nature I'd
Smell of pemmican and trees

I remember canoeing with my
Girlfriend in the vast wilderness
Of Quetico

The sky perfectly blue
The lake perfectly smooth

The air suddenly suffused with the
Sweet smell of my girlfriend's skin

My guess is, they must have thought
We were *Windigo*

The way we devoured the land and
Sucked in their kids

Taught them French and English and
Cut out their native tongues

If, through my magic window, I could
Return to that once-in-a-lifetime day

I'd open my *windigo* mouth
And swallow the world

Temagami

That night we made love where a tree had
Fallen and crushed a moose

The only campsite on this tiny lily-pad lake

Thank God the wind was blowing the other
Way while I hauled our packs past the decay

Chopped wood while you made a fire
Set up the tent while you cooked supper

Afterwards read a story out loud while a red
Squirrel inched down a tree

And squeezed into the space between my
Back and the log I was leaning against

Its little inquisitive head poking out from
Under my arm before it fell asleep

Inukshuk

Seventy-five, half-blind, going slowly deaf

Nevertheless, on the magic side of my magic
Window, I am *coureur de bois*

My eyesight keen
My body lithe

My moccasins gliding across the forest floor
Without disturbing a twig

My feet so soundless I surprise a man with
His back to me

He is on his knees, balancing one stone on
Top of another

He is rebuilding the *inukshuk* in our woods

For years I've seen its stones knocked over
Only to see it raised again

And for years I've wondered who its secret
Guardian was

Now I know

His name is Detrik
An electrician

Lives on my dirt road
Four houses down

Blond, blue-eyed, fair-skinned

Not the shaman I expected to see this side
Of my magic window

He turns, sees me, shrugs self-consciously

Then lifts a head-shaped rock and sets it
On the shoulder stones below

Gypsy Moths

Spent this morning patrolling a path
Which an army or gypsy moths was
Crossing near my home

Me doing a Cape Breton step dance
Crushing so many my Birkenstocks
Were slippery with their slime

Afterwards, having slathered my
Maple trees with Vaseline, I scraped
The trapped insects onto a tarpaulin

Then funneled them into a bucket of
Hot, soapy water

Must have been thousands

Me exulting in the plan's execution
Its scientific precision

Of course, there are always a few
Recalcitrants

A few still holding onto the tarpaulin
Or twisting this way and that on the lip
Of the bucket

Before I flick them in

Synesthesia

I loved 1967 because I was 21 and
I loved making love, not war

I loved sitting in a circle on the floor
While holding my breath and passing
Around a joint

I loved the sweet, acrid smell

And the way rain on a windowpane
Could look like cartoon characters
Sliding down a hill

The way one night, high on Moroccan
Kief, notes of music suddenly became
Rectangular panes of colour hanging
In the air

Synesthesia, it's called

The way a woman's voice becomes the smell
Of her long black hair

Becomes the feel of her skin on your tongue

I loved the Sixties because it seemed everyone
I knew was an artist of some kind

No babies yet or hearing aids or fears of going
Blind

All of us in a circle throwing the *I Ching*

None of us seeing clearly what the future
Would bring

Flaws

In Nepal, monks create their holy
Art with grains of coloured sand

Then sweep them to the wind

In Isfahan, imperfection is woven into
Every rug

Lest God be moved to jealous wrath

While Navajos weave their rugs with
Loving flaws

To let gods in and let them out

As for me, I make mistakes for no
God-given reason

Even my failings are not as perfect
As they could be

Everton

You've got to love an old guy like Everton
Even though he's an alcoholic and morose
In the morning

But if you shut up and leave him alone
Hand him tools when he's on the ladder
Make him a cup of coffee

After a while he loosens up

You see them cracks?

He's pointing at two cracks, one on either
Side of my picture window

I could mud them and sand them and
You'd think I done a good job. But two
Maybe three years from now, there they'd
Be again

His lips curl in disgust

It's lucky for me, he says, he's been taping
Drywall for fifty years

Lucky for me he knows his business

For cracks like that you got to use a
Special kind of mud

Lucky for me, he's got some in his truck

The next morning the sanding begins
Dust everywhere, drifting down on his
Eyebrows, greying his skin

I make him another cup of coffee

He tells me he's going to retire at the
End of the month

Back to Jamaica
His sister's place

I google the address he gives me and
We stare at the street view of her house

Lemon yellow walls, green shutters, blue
Railings around the porch

Yeah, just gonna put my feet up and sit
There with a long, tall glass of rum

Lucky for me, he says, my living room
Will be the last reno he ever does

Got to give you my best, he says

All the cracks filled
All the joints taped
Walls sanded smooth and straight

If he does it all perfectly, he says, when
The walls are painted, his work will be
Invisible

Ain't Nothing

Ain't nothing like thoughts of death
To get your juices flowing
Ain't nothing like a dearth of breath
To remind a mind it's slowing

There's nothing like a spotted hand
To make you see how dots connect
Nothing like the life you planned
To make you see your future wreck

So much to do, so little time
Forget your perfect word, your rhyme
A perfect poem, like a perfect crime
If ever done would leave no sign

Be content to be forgot
In the end it matters not

Cornflowers

I don't know their proper name, but
We called them cornflowers

Five or six on a thin, green stem

They looked like daisies somebody had
Painted a faded blue jeans blue

They were always there in June when I
Got out of school and roamed the fields
Around my boyhood home

And now here they were again, growing
Beside this old man's path in Ontario

Me, leaning forward on my cane, saying
I appreciated them coming all the way
From Quebec

And looking round to make sure no one
Thought me crazy, I whispered how much
I'd always loved them even as a child

This Walk

I love this walk which once, perhaps
Was an Iroquois track through woods
So thick not even a shaman could see
The railroad coming

The one that ran here for a hundred
Years past farmers' stump-cleared
Fields and the log tents they put up
Over square, stone-sided holes

All this before highways and trucks
Made this railroad obsolete

Now, the ties and rails torn out, I walk
My dogs along this country path

I believe they like the fact it is always
The same path, though it changes with
The seasons – ice, sludge, flood, mud

How, at the moment, it is smooth and dry

I notice the eldest has begun lagging and
No longer comes running when I call

I don't mind
I know the symptoms well

I use the time to yank a strangling vine
From an apple tree

Walk slowly among chokecherries and
Waterfalls of wild Canadian grapes

I have tasted them all and plucked poems
Here from the ancient air

In the far distance, the path bends and is
Screened by trees

I can tell my dog is tired and I have no
Desire to walk there either

Me and My Shadow

This trail I'm on must be aimed due
East

The sun, setting behind me, pushes
My shadow dead ahead

The lower the sun, the longer the
Shadow

Almost alien now: distorted head
On elongated neck

Arms, shoulders, legs impossibly
Ethereally thin

It strides in front of me as if trying
To get away from this old geezer's
Plodding steps

As if eager to plunge into the world
Darkening around me

So I stomp on its feet and keep it
Pinned down

Like my mother, me muttering under
My breath, "Not yet! Not yet!"

Except she was shouting, sitting bolt
Upright in bed, her heart stopped

Banging her chest with her fist, trying
To get it started again

It's Its Silence

It's its silence that scares me
And reminds me of my mother

The way, mouth open, she lay
On the gurney

Before they wheeled her into
The flames

And there was no scream

It's its silence that scares me
Like the last rose of summer

How still it still stands, pink
And demure

While its petals unblossom
And fall to the ground

Here, in this silence, time moves
Slowly but never slows down

Ruth

My mother-in-law is 95

We rescued her just before
COVID turned the whole
World into a nursing home

Her mind is sharp but there
Are cracks in her vertebrae

And growths in her kidneys

So she is in pain and waiting
For it to end

She and her husband were
Majors in the Salvation Army

Spent their lives doing God's
Good work

Without a trace of hypocrisy
Or selfishness

Moving from one ministry to
Another, moving from city to city
Moving from home to home

Now, to pass the time, my wife
Sits beside her doing crosswords

If her back didn't hurt so much
Ruth would rather be hunched over
A picture puzzle

Instead, she pretends interest in
The TV news I am watching
About COVID and vaccines

None of it mattering much

There being no disease in the home
Ruth has been moving to all along

On Turning Seventy-Nine

When I recall how distant my father could be
I remember my friend Anthony leaning against
His father's knee, the father's hand stroking
Anthony's head so lovingly

The gesture so natural, so spontaneous
I burst into tears

Now, sitting on my porch and patting my cat
I feel the stirrings of a warm summer breeze
And wait for a winter's wind to ruffle my hair

Après moi, le déluge

One of the great pleasures in this old man's
Life is watching the rain

Me standing on my porch smoking a cigarette

I know, I know… But at my age what difference
Does it make

Friends and people much younger than myself
Dropping like the rain all around me, dropping
Like flies

Btw, did you know that Beelzebub is Hebrew for
Lord of the Flies, a book I taught for 20 years and
Never grew tired of

Watching row upon row of innocent eyes grow
Wide as its meaning sank in – one of the many
Pleasures I used to have and now miss

So I smoke a cigarette and watch the rain flooding
The dirt road in front of my house, listen to its
Hammering against the roof

I see a flash of lightning and count the seconds
Before the thunder comes shaking the world like
One of those gods I wish I could believe in

Me thrilled to think this might be it, this might be
The final reckoning, the deluge Louis the Fifteenth
Wanted to miss

The idiot! I'd give my right arm and both my
Slowly dimming eyes to see the splendour of
His raiment in the midst of this black firmament

But the sky clears and returns to a blue more
Faded than the blue I remember as a kid

My wife, pointing to flowers shattered by the
Storm, saying how beautiful they had been

What Began as a Wobble

What began as a wobble in
A telephone pole became a
Blind spot at the centre of
My vision

Wet AMD, the doctor said

And what began as a cancer
On my nose was replaced by
Its red oozing twin on my
Forehead

Then reappeared as blood
In my urine and a lump in
My bladder

Lucky we caught it early
The doctor said

Now what began as an aching
Back has become a tingling all
The way to my knee

Sciatica, my doctor says

Life dribbling away
Death pissing down my leg

Something Wrong

One thing I have always loved is sitting
In a restaurant with a cup of coffee and
A cigarette

Reading, say, *L'Étranger*, by Albert
Camus, in the original French

(I'm bragging here)

Or *Tropic of Cancer*, by Henry Miller
In the original uncensored English

For me, pure happiness

It was only later, much later, when
They banned smoking in restaurants
That my happiness was diminished

But, by then, I was legally blind and
Could not even watch TV, let alone
Decipher wriggling spider legs of type

It took half a decade more before my
Sight, restored by modern meds, was
Good enough to let me read again

I remember that miraculous moment
When I turned to the first page of the
First book I'd bought in years

Obviously, something wrong

A grown man sitting in a restaurant
With a cup of coffee and no cigarette

The book fallen from his hands, tears
Falling on the tabletop

The Eyes Have It

I loved my eyes when I was young
The world they saw was clear
The future then a mystery
The present then a mirror

I loved my eyes when I was young
The breasts and thighs they saw
A lover's' smile could fool me then
Took time to see the flaw

How strange! That world has disappeared
Has darkened, greyed and dimmed
The past is now the mystery
The future clear and grim

It Breaks My Heart

It breaks my heart to see my wife grow old
Those lips I kissed, that waist I loved to hold
Her hair now somehow traded, bought, swapped, sold
For silver where before was reddish gold

It breaks my heart to see her eyes grow dim
Light glinting on her reading glasses' rim
Her girlish laugh become a weary grin
Age a stain on her skin's enameling

It even breaks my heart to have her near
To have her speak the words I long to hear
That she will love me bald, while from my ears
And nostrils sprout more hairs than I have years

Yes, it breaks my heart to see much nearer
My own slow aging, her face my mirror

Winter Solstice

Yes, a cup of coffee and a cigarette
That's what it comes down to

When it's half past three
In the morning

And you find yourself walking to
The river at the end of your yard

Singing softly to the silent world

To fish swimming under ice and
Rabbits tunnelling under snow

You can't see them but it makes
You happy to know they're there

Yes, that's what it comes down to
The darkest night of the year

Dead of Winter

I love the dead of winter

Especially here in these woods
Where the trunks of trees
Look like a herd of frozen
Elephants

I love the way, against a winter
Sky, a tree's thin black limbs look
Like cracks in a windshield

Or, when snow sticks to them
How they look like shocked old
Ladies with frizzled hair

In the dead of winter, the snow is
So hard your boots do not sink in
And you can walk across a field
In any direction

In the dead of winter there are no
Paths

In the dead of winter, you can stop
On your way to the top of a hill

Or, here in these woods, you can
Just be very, very still

Winter Rain

This is Ontario
So there's no way to know
Whether this freezing rain
Will stay and turn to snow
Or simply melt away

And this is mid-winter
The coldest time of year
When an unshovelled path
Can turn to ice so sheer
I slip and fall and yearn

For that January
Long gone, when I buried
My nose in your perfumed
Coat – your answering squeeze
A teenage game of grope

Before we played for keeps
And fell asleep in sheets
As warm, love-wrinkled and
Worn as this old man's cheeks
In freezing rain and storm

In Praise of My Country

What I like about Canada
Is what I love about my wife

Her astonishing natural beauty

I have swum in the lakes of her
Eyes

Pitched my tent in the crook
Of her arm

Portaged my canoe from vein
To vein

Many times I have tramped up
The hill of a knee

And seen the winter drift of her
Snow-white skin, the vast continent
Of her summer smile

O Canada! Across your mountains
And your valleys I have journeyed

To all the far-off corners of my bed

At the Top of the Hill

Aside from the cross you make at the
Top of the hill when you turn your skis
The best thing about x-country skiing is
The long wild effortless ride all the way
Down to where you started

Knees bent, not moving a muscle, poles
No longer needed, you hurtle forward
Towards that rush of weightlessness you
Know you long for

How quickly you forget the uphill climb
The wheezing in your chest, the wind
Whipping round your ears, the snow erasing
Any trace of where you've been

My Shepherds

When we go on our long walks across
Snow-covered hills, Blue sometimes
Wanders off

That is when Saga races back to find
Her while I stand stamping my feet in
The cold

Otherwise, Saga is usually far ahead
Scouting from left to right to left

Ready to defend against wolves and
Sheep-stealing thieves

I wonder if they worry our pack is too
Small, just the three of us in this world
Of white

And me the only one who knows where
We are going

Nunchucks

Eventually every antelope slows down

Becomes the one looking at the lion
Leaping toward it from behind

Eventually the lion slows down

Jaw broken by a zebra's hoof, spine
Broken by brothers of another pride

There has been a sudden thaw and Saga
Returns with the leg bones of a deer

Femur and tibia still held together by
Their ligaments

Nature's nunchucks

Whirling them above my head, I turn and
Crush the skull of a lion leaping towards
Me from behind

Ouroboros

When I think of us as living dust
Circling the sun, I think of the
Trilobites whose bodies became
The rocks of the Rockies

I think of us as the paddle-finned fish
Who waded ashore while all around
Seaweed became air-breathing trees

And when at last there was oxygen enough
I think of a rabbit screaming in a coyote's
Mouth and wolves chasing deer through
Lush, green fields

Circling streaks of blood-warmed dust
We weigh our lives on a serpent's scale
And tell a story that swallows its tale

This Life I'm Leaving

I love this life I'm leaving
That's the trochee long and short of it
The iambic short and long of it
Though measureless my grieving

I salute spring's muddy best
This host of dactyl daffodils
Though darling buds of May may bless
Mosquitoes and other anapests

Enough! No pun is worth
My death; no joke can wake the dead
Some spring the earth's rebirth
Will mud my grinning head

I love winter, summer, fall
But April is the cruelest love of all

Instead

I thought I'd sing a song of love
Instead I wrote of pain
I thought I'd praise my younger days
Instead I watched them wane

I thought, instead of discontent
I'd sing of harmony
I never meant a long lament
Of such solemnity

I'm sorry if these winter lines
Engrave your summer eyes
Old age will change you too in time
And won't apologize

If death's the end of life's design
I walk downhill each step I climb

9/11, The Last Word

To sing another villanelle
We choke on dust and conquer thirst
At the bottom of this well

No fitter rhyme could this tale tell
For we, though last, are not the first
To sing another villanelle

When towers burned in sky-high hell
We found ourselves, our world, reversed
At the bottom of this well

When lovers jumped and others fell
Our parched hearts yearned before they burst
To sing another villanelle

That sidewalk thump will sound our knell
Unless that sound, in art, is nursed
At the bottom of this well

Though words can never death dispel
I raise my voice in verse unhearsed
To sing another villanelle
At the bottom of this well

Acknowledgements

As always, I owe a debt of unrepayable gratitude to my stepmother, Aviva, as well as to my best friend, Stephanie, and to my wife, Sharon, for the many hours spent reading these lines and making suggestions for improvement. Thanks, too, as always, to my friend and fellow poet, Robert Priest, not only for his artistic example but also for his advice. In addition, I owe a posthumous thank you to Stephanie's late father, Gordon Rayner Sr., for using me as the model for one of his Harlequin cover illustrations. And finally, speaking of fathers, I owe the deepest debt of all to my father, Irving Layton, for the example he set for me of a poet dedicated to his task. May these poems be worthy of all the help I have received over the years!

In addition, the author wishes to thank the editor of *Freefall* for publishing "Après Moi, Le Dèluge" (Volume 26, No. 2) and the editor of *The Café Review* for publishing "Instead" and "This Life I'm Leaving" (Volume 35, Winter 2024)

Finally, the author acknowledges the financial support of the Ontario Arts Council.

About the Author

Born in Montreal in 1946, the eldest son of poet Irving Layton and artist Betty Sutherland, a.k.a. Boschka, Max left home when he was 16 and survived by working as everything from tobacco picker and logger to bookstore owner, bank vice president, and high school English teacher. Along the way he earned a BA in Philosophy at Concordia and an MA in English Literature at the University of Toronto. A published novelist and short story writer (Mosaic Press), Max was diagnosed with Age-related Macular Degeneration (AMD) and was legally blind for several years. It was during this time, after 9/11, that he recorded the first of four CDs of original songs and wrote the first of his three subsequent books of poetry (all published by Guernica Editions). His eyesight restored thanks to the miracle of modern science, but now diagnosed with multiple myeloma, Max lives on the banks of the Credit River in southern Ontario with his wife, Sharon. For more information about Max, go to www.maxlayton.com.

ALSO BY MAX LAYTON

Poetry

LIKE
In The Garden Of I Am
When The Rapture Comes

A novel

Some Kind Of Hero

Short Stories

Objects In Mirror Are Closer Than They Appear

CDs

True The North
It's A Mystery To Me
2 The Max
Heartbeat Of Time

Printed by Imprimerie Gauvin
Gatineau, Québec